Loving aı

Alzheimer's:

A Reflection

Loving and Living with Alzheimer's:

A Reflection

By

Jerilyn Tyner

Kindle Direct Publishing

Copyright © 2022 *Jerilyn Tyner*

ISBN: 9798796056127

First edition

Cover Photography: Mark James

Back cover portrait: Life At A Glance Photography, Shelli Olin

Co-publisher: Dawn Wriglesworth

jerilyntyner@gmail.com

@ WriteAwayBooks

All scripture quotations from Authorized King James Version

Thank You

This book is dedicated to every person who stood by me with a shoulder to lean on and a hand to hold as Tom and I walked our six-year journey through Alzheimer's disease.

Additional thanks to Dawn Wriglesworth for help with publishing and Mark James for use of the cover photograph.

ABOUT THIS BOOK

Loving, and Living with Alzheimer's: A Reflection is about the hard road of caring for a loved one who has been diagnosed with a frightening disease. It is in no way intended to give medical or professional advice, but simply a candid chronicle of the experience of one wife whose love for her husband carried her through the hardships and blessings of a six-year journey. It is offered to the reader with the hope that it might encourage you to know that whatever trial you are facing, there is hope in walking hand in hand with God and keeping love alive. I hope as you read these pages, you will feel that you have met a friend. I welcome you to contact me at: jerilyntyner@gmail.com

I fell in love when I was 19 years old. Summertime, of course. A new guy had come to town, planning to attend the same local college where I was about to begin my junior year as an elementary education major. One Sunday night he came to our church youth group and as I sat at the piano getting my music ready for the singing, I heard our advisor introducing some guy to the other kids.

It's hard to explain what happened next. I heard a voice in my head saying, "The guy you are going to marry just walked in this room."

I turned and looked. I turned back around. *I heard nothing!* I told myself. He just didn't look like my type. In fact, he didn't look like anybody I knew. He was skinny. He had a very short haircut, and he wore glasses with black frames. He reminded me of Buddy Holly. And he talked with a funny New York accent. Not my type. I started playing the intro for the first song.

Before long, this guy (whose name was Tom) had become friends with my cousin Paul who was living with my family that summer, and my girlfriend and I got in the habit of hanging out with the two of them in the evenings. We played cards, went to the Dairy Queen for ice cream, and lounged around in our screened in porch to avoid the mosquitos. We talked about a lot of things, and (of course) he had lots of stories about living in upstate New York. He had a "gift of gab," and kept us laughing at his stories,

11

especially the tale of his trip from New York to Florida on a Vespa motor scooter with his friend Mike Bacon. It wasn't just his stories that kept us laughing. He had a quirky way of looking at everyday life that made living fun.

One night he was lying on the sofa and I was sitting across from him in a chair.

As usual, we were all in stitches over his latest joke. *He is so cute! He is sooo cute!* As this thought went through my mind, I had the feeling that little hearts were circling around my head like they do in the comic strips when the girl is falling in love. I caught my breath. *Oh, my goodness. I hope no one can see them.*

From then on, something was happening.

One night he and I went for a ride together. Just the two of us. It wasn't a date, because I had a casual boyfriend (who was working nights) whom I had been dating for the past few months. *Tom and I are just friends, hanging out. Going for a ride. Going to the park and feeding the ducks. And I am certainly NOT going to let him kiss me.*

An odd thing happened. We kept passing cars that only had one headlight, and he kept calling "Puh-diddle!" There was (in those long-past days) a game about cars with one headlight. If a person called puh-diddle first, the other person had to give a kiss, or get punched if it was the same sex person. (Sort of like the *Jinx, you owe me a Coke* routine.)

Of course, I kept refusing to "pay" the kiss, and stayed far away on the other side of the front seat of his '52 Studebaker. The

12

evening was beautiful, filled with stars and with love songs playing on the radio. (Think "I Wanna Hold Your Haaaand," or "There, I've Said It Again.") We fed the ducks, walked around the quiet park, and swayed dreamily on the swings. On the way back to my house, we passed another one-eyed car. He pulled up in front of my house, and turned off the car.

"Come on," he teased. "You've got to pay up for at least one of those puh-diddles."

My heart gave a little jump. *That might be nice.* "Oh, all right." I scooted across the seat, and he kissed me.

He opened the door on the driver's side and started to get out. He had one foot out the door.

"Is that all," I said.

"Not if you don't want it to be." With a gleam in his eye, he shut the car door, took off his Buddy Holly glasses, hung them on the rear-view mirror, and collected the rest of the kisses.

A year later, we were married.

Now, I'm sure some of you are thinking, "What? I thought this book was supposed to be about Alzheimer's. What does a corny story about a couple of teenagers have to do with anything?"

Yes, we were just kids with not much life experience and even less preparation for a lifetime commitment. But young love is real. We took those vows of better or worse, richer or poorer, sickness or health and soon found out relationships are hard. But through the years, we also learned going through hard times and not giving up cements the love in an unbreakable bond.

Notice in the title of this book there is a comma after *Loving*. You see, if you don't have the loving part, the journey through Alzheimer's disease is going to be more painful than you can handle. As I have become the caregiver of my husband through this difficult disease, I often have to remind myself that he's Tom. The guy with the funny accent, the great sense of humor, and the warm, exciting kisses. And it gives me courage to love another day in another way.

FOR THOUGHT, JOURNALING, OR SHARING

How did you and your loved one meet? What were some of the qualities that attracted you to him/her as a person. Think of a special memory that keeps you going on hard days.

WHAT'S GOING ON?

Either he is crazy, or I am! We were close to celebrating our fiftieth wedding anniversary. Our four sons were all adults, married to wonderful women and raising kids of their own. We had recently retired, gone through a downsizing, and moved into a two-bedroom apartment. I was feeling very unsure about the next chapter of our lives, and even more so as I noticed distinct changes in Tom's behavior. Even the way he talked was different. Kind of fragmented. Not being able to find the word for a common object. Getting irritable over small happenings. Doing things that did not make sense.

"Either he is crazy, or I am." I thought as I picked up the receiver and dialed my doctor's office. I know as people hit their "senior years" they can expect "senior moments."

"Now, why did I come into this room?"

"What day of the week is this? Have I forgotten my dentist appointment?"

"Shoot! I forgot to bring the dessert I made for the potluck. I'll have to drive home and get it, and then I'll be late."

And of course, men have their "moments" too, but my husband's behavior had been much more serious. Making a sandwich, leaving PBJ open on the counter and walking off forgetting to eat it. Leaving his work tools on the job site. Not knowing where our children lived. Unable to find the word for a common, everyday object. Overall difficulty to express his thoughts. Irritation with himself and with me.

One night we were on our way home from a meeting, driving through the town we had lived in for twenty-some years. "Where are we?" he cried out, jerking the wheel. Then he freaked out and hit the meridian between the lanes. Off flew the hubcap from the front wheel, but he kept driving without slowing down and went through a red light.

It was time to get a professional opinion, so after much hesitation; I made the appointment with his primary care doctor who had known us for years. Tom was very good at making first impressions, and would never admit to having any problems, and lately if anything went awry, he implied it was my fault. I decided to be proactive, so I made a list of the behaviors that were concerning me and sent it to the doctor's office. (I kept a copy for my records, but now I can't remember where I put it. I also have senior moments.)

The appointment began with the usual questions and Tom's assurances that he was doing fine. I said nothing. Eventually, the doctor brought in his assistant to give the now-famous mini-mental test, asking generic questions such as birthdate, age, season, who's the President, where are you now, what's the day of the week, what city/county are you in, etc. He missed over half the answers. Another part of the test was remembering three words—in this case, Apple, Table, Penny—for a few minutes and then repeating them when asked. He couldn't do it. He was given a paper and asked to copy a geometric shape, which was no problem for him as a construction pro, and to write a sentence, which he also did. Still, he had a low enough score to warrant a referral to a psychologist for complete testing.

The process was threefold: 1. An interview with both of us about his history; 2. A day of psychological testing which I did not participate in; 3. A discussion with the psychologist about the results. Part three was the hardest. Because he had a similar battery of tests several years earlier (after he had been struck by lightning ... that's another story) and I had kept the results, the psychologist had a baseline for comparison. She was gentle, but plainspoken. He had frontal-temporal dementia that was severely affecting his memory.

Alzheimer's disease and dementia are two different things. Dementia is more of a general condition. It includes a wide range of symptoms that are serious enough to make everyday life hard to manage, whereas Alzheimer's is one of the most common diseases that cause dementia. The distinction can be confusing. Both are scary words no one wants to hear.

My heart sank. I had found out what I suspected was true, but I didn't want it to be so.

We were both very quiet on the ride home. I could tell he was having a hard time taking in the diagnosis. I watched his face as the color drained his usually ruddy complexion. With tears in his voice he spoke.

"I'm sorry, Jerilyn."

My heart broke.

This was nothing we planned on, nothing we expected, and nothing we could have done anything to prevent. It was as if in a flash he had glimpsed the road ahead and was consumed by sorrow.

I will never forget that moment. I think of it now, some six years after the diagnosis. Our doctor recommended a book for me called *The Thirty-six Hour Day,* and it is a fitting title of the wearying days and confusing nights for both of us as his abilities decline and my patience grows thin. I never doubt how much he loves me. I know he would do anything in the world to keep me from the weight and worry his illness brings to our life, and that knowledge is enough to banish resentment and keep caring for him the best way I can, even if it is a Thirty Six Hour Day.

FOR THOUGHT, JOURNALING, OR SHARING

How do you decide when your loved one needs a professional evaluation? Is there anything to be gained by waiting until the situation reaches a crisis level? How might you deal with stubborn resistance or plain refusal to seek diagnosis?

"I know I can do this," I tell myself. "I love this man, and the vows we took 50 years ago are still in force. For better or for worse doesn't change when the trail gets bumpy." And the trail does get bumpy. Right away. No one sees it but me, because he still looks pretty good from the outside. My hubby has always been an extrovert—a people person—and that hasn't changed. At parties, at church, at family events he's still fun to be around. Even when we're in line at the grocery store, he'll strike up a conversation with a stranger who'll soon be laughing along with Tom. Even though at times he says something that doesn't make sense, if I tell a close friend about his diagnosis, she'll say, "Really? I would never have guessed that. He seems perfectly normal." I sometimes joke, "Actually he's never been perfectly normal," and change the subject.

No one else knows the daily changes and challenges. Bumps. I climb over them with a smile, and remind myself, "I can do this."

I find myself correcting his mistakes and inaccurate "memories." I joke. "He has a great memory. He even remembers things that never happened."

I soon learn not to correct his stories and ideas. When people have Alzheimer's, their conception of reality is changed, and trying to convince them otherwise hurts and confuses them. Even if you do manage to persuade them they are wrong, they

21

won't remember accurately the next time. It is best to be gentle. After all, they are not giving testimony under oath in a courtroom.

I take up all the responsibility for family finances even though that's definitely not my strong point, and struggle with resentment when correcting his mistakes. I grow increasingly irritated by his constantly losing his keys, his wallet, his hat, and leaving something behind everywhere we go. He has four or five winter jackets at various places throughout the county.

I am confused about the changing roles in our relationship. Am I his wife or his caregiver? His lover or his parent?

Eventually, someone suggests that I join a support group for Alzheimer's caregivers, so I make the call and go to the group. There are four or five people there, each with a different life situation, and a facilitator who has tons of helpful information but has never lived with a dementia patient. The people don't bond. Every month there are different people there, and some never come back.

At this time, the biggest bump in my path is the matter of Tom's driving. It has become erratic and he sometimes forgets where he's going. Some "friend" of ours decides he's going to do me a favor and reports to the authorities that Tom is an unsafe driver. (I never even knew a person could do that. Did you?) Tom gets a notice from the DOL that he has to come in and take the written test, and after passing it, take a road test. Until he does that, his license is suspended.

He is outraged. "I'm a good driver," he yells. "How dare they try to take my license?"

I don't argue. "That's fine," I answer. "Then all you have to do is go down and take the test and get your license back. Here's the rules of the road book they sent you. Do you want to study it before you go?"

He picks it up, thumbs through a few pages, and tosses it aside. "I know this stuff. Let's go."

At the bureau, he is chagrined to find out the written test is no longer really written. It's computerized. His computer skills are limited to playing games, and in less than ten minutes he has failed the test. The lady tells him not to worry. He can study for it and come back again. I also tell him I believe he can request to take the test on paper, rather than computer, but it never works out for him. He continues to drive the car anyway.

I know this must not continue, so I share this problem with the support group. The facilitator immediately freaks out and tells me I have to take his keys away and stop him from driving, even if it's only a three-block drive to Safeway. She does not know my husband. The chances of my preventing him from doing something he has made up his mind to do are nonexistent. I know this from 50 years of living with him. The next month, she returns to the topic and replays the broken record.

"I thought this was a support group," I say. "You are supposed to support me in my struggle, not nag me about what you think I should do. I know he is going to have to stop driving, but how I handle it is my decision."

I'm not saying my experience is typical. I attended several workshops sponsored by the organization and received a wealth of helpful resources. Many people find the information and connections through the Alzheimer's Association very valuable, but this particular group didn't happen to be the right thing for me. That's the last meeting I attend.

Before long, I gradually take over the driving, and he is satisfied to be a passenger as long as I let him tell me to speed up or slow down, where to park, and to stop or go when the light changes. I feel irritated, but I keep reminding myself it's just another bump and I can handle it.

But I can't. As his memory declines, I find myself being depressed and irritable, and it doesn't help that I lie awake half the night.

As I chase my worries around my brain, a Bible verse comes to my mind. *"Without Me, you can do nothing."* (John 13:5b)

Oh. Maybe my insistence that I can handle it all myself is actually conceit. God doesn't mean for any of us to do it all. He provides the help we need if we are humble enough to ask for it and allow others to share our pain. I pray about it. I share with my loving and supportive family God brings people alongside who have also experienced the devastation of Alzheimer's. I am also blessed with some good friends who are trustworthy, nonjudgmental, and kind. Most of all, they are good listeners. I feel safe sharing my feelings with them, and somehow the bumpy trail is easier to travel.

FOR THOUGHT, JOURNALING OR SHARING

Is it easy or hard for you to ask for help? How important do you think it is to have a support network, and who do you think should be included in that group? How will you know when it's time for your loved one to stop driving, and who will support your decision?

"Do you have a DPOA?" the social worker asked me.

"Umm. What's that? I don't think so."

I was soon to find out those letters stand for Durable Power of Attorney. Something I'd never heard of, or if I did, I must have ignored it. I have very selective hearing, and I seldom pay attention to what's coming in the future because I'm too occupied with the right now.

I soon learned that we needed to complete several health care planning documents that would require help from doctors and lawyers. Contacting the doctor would be no problem since we were both due for checkups. It was a simple matter to complete the POLST form, which stands for Physician's Orders for Life Sustaining Treatment. We had talked about our wishes and neither of us wanted to have CPR if we were not breathing and had no pulse. We checked the DNR box. Nor did we desire intubation or mechanical ventilation. When the Lord called us home to heaven, we were ready to go. We discussed these matters with the doctor and he signed the forms which we took home and posted on the side of the refrigerator. They are on bright green paper, and easy to find.

As for the legal documents we needed a lawyer to prepare, that was a different matter. Should I look up the number of a lawyer in our town and make an appointment? Maybe we could put that off for a while longer. And a while longer becomes longer and longer until you almost forget a task you really don't want to face anyway.

While I was procrastinating, a sign showed up on the bulletin board in the mail room of our apartment complex. A legal team was coming to our building for the very purpose of preparing end of life documents including a Living Will, a General Durable Power of Attorney, a DPOA for health care, and estate planning or will. Everything we needed. But how much would it cost to have these documents prepared and notarized?

Not one dollar. These good people were offering their professional services *pro bono*. Of course, we signed up for an appointment and went through the process very painlessly and properly. I filed the documents in a safe place and sighed in relief. I knew hard decisions would still need to be made as Tom's disease progressed, but it was a good feeling to be ready with the needed paperwork.

I knew it had been a godsend.

It may not seem miraculous to others, but I saw it as evidence of God's grace that we were in the right place at the time to receive this blessing. You see, I had been angry and depressed when we moved here. We had left behind the home we had lived in for over twenty years. It didn't seem fair to me that we had to move into an apartment and thus be forced to get rid of many things that were important to me. Downsizing is hard, especially if it isn't your choice. The move might have been out of my control, but it certainly wasn't out of God's design. He always has our best in mind. I am ashamed now of the attitude I had and my lack of faith in Him. Somehow, the experience with the legal documents caught my attention, and I began to see God's provision and plan in many ways I had been blind to in my stubbornness.

It was shortly after we moved that Tom was diagnosed with Alzheimer's. The signs were waving even before we moved. One of the early markers is difficulty doing tasks that have been previously accomplished easily. For example, when the lawn needed mowing, he would start up the mower, mow a few rounds, quit, and leave the mower in the middle of the yard, never to return. He now found simple household repairs daunting. He forgot how to do things that had been second nature to him and became frustrated over the simplest jobs.

It was a blessing that the yard work, building maintenance, and even apartment repairs were now covered in our rent. If the garbage disposal got plugged, the maintenance guy magically repaired it. When the dishwasher stopped working, he wheeled in a new one the next day and Tom didn't even have to hook it up.

Alzheimer's patients also lose their ability to plan and participate in social activities. Here, we had an abundance of friendly people ready to play a card game, go for a walk, share a potluck supper, or just sit and visit. Best of all, there was always someone who needed a hand moving furniture, carrying in groceries that were too heavy, hanging a picture, or just sitting down and chatting for a while. *Voila!* A ready-made social program.

29

Although Tom never smoked, he often went outside in the morning and wiped the moisture or rain off the benches so his friends who smoked would have a dry place to sit down. And he and our dog would sit down with them and "chit-chat" as he said.

I have already mentioned that as Tom's disabilities became more evident, the neighbors were kind and understanding and looked out for him in many ways.

Best of all, after we had lived here a while, we found the church where we were welcomed and have been continually blessed with fellowship and godly teaching.

How often it has been said, God's ways are not our ways, but how kind he is. What God gives is always best. He sends the sun and the rain, the light and the dark. All love is from him. It doesn't have to be Thanksgiving Day to be grateful.

FOR THOUGHT, JOURNALING, OR SHARING

How has God worked in your circumstances to assure you that He wants what is best for you and is working all things for your good? (Romans 8:28) Thank Him for all His blessings.

It's for sure that declining mental abilities are at the heart of living with Alzheimer's disease, but physical changes become challenging also. My first new task was medication management. Ever since I'd met Tom, he was independent in every way. He had few medications, but whatever pills he did have he managed on his own. Gradually, I had to remind him daily, then check up on him, remind him, and finally put the medicine in his hand and watch him swallow it with a gulp of water. Not so hard, right?

Though we were handling the minor changes fairly well, one summer's day we came to a treacherous curve.

He had a heart attack.

On Sunday morning he wasn't feeling well. I suggested we stay home from church, but he wanted to go. When he got out of the car I noticed beads of perspiration on his forehead. But it was a hot day, after all. During the service he looked a little grayish and was breathing hard. Still, I was shocked when he collapsed as the pastor was giving the benediction. I wonder what the preacher thought when his parishioner keeled over in the aisle as he pronounced the final "Amen." It must have been a powerful sermon, right?

Pastor Ryan rushed down the aisle, and a doctor in the congregation came quickly over. After assessing his condition, they sent for the ambulance and he was taken to the hospital and admitted. He had indeed had a "cardiac event," or what we call a heart attack.

The next morning I was sitting on a hard bench in a small waiting room when the doctor came in. It was mid-August and I had been awake over 24 hours. "Your husband has a blood clot in his aorta," he told me. "He's had a mild heart attack. He will be okay, but we need to keep him here until he's stable."

He began to feel better after a few days, but he was very mixed up and didn't recall or understand what had happened to him. He said, "When I woke up in the church, there were three nurses standing around me in white dresses." He also said, "I was in a hospital with a lot of military guys there who needed blood transfusions. They kept taking my blood and giving it to the officers because I had the right type of blood."

I didn't try to talk him out of these ideas because I thought it would just make him more stressed. Besides, what did it matter? Maybe what he'd seen as nurses were angels in white, or instead of military men, heavenly warriors in the hospital halls. I quickly learned it is not necessary or helpful to correct your spouse who has dementia. What they say is their reality, and it only distresses them more if you argue with them. Most likely, they won't remember it anyway.

Three days later he was sent home by the cardiologist with medications for the patient and instructions for me to administer them and take care of Tom.

33

Some meds he had been taking were discontinued, and others were added. After picking up everything from the pharmacy, I sat at the kitchen table with pages of instructions and descriptions of scary side effects, a collection of pill bottles, and a plastic container with sections for each day of the week, five times a day—morning, mid-morning, noon, dinner time, and bedtime. Each medication had an unpronounceable name and varied dosages and times. It was all Greek to me. Or was it Latin?

I was jittery as a wild hare. I've had no medical training other than what I learned in first aid class and in taking care of four rowdy boys. How would I, with my scatter-brained approach to life, ever get it right? I've never felt more insecure in my wifely role and never more uncertain of the future, but I knew family and friends were praying for us.

One day I fell into an exhausted sleep that lasted a couple of hours and woke myself up singing. It was an old melody: *"I don't know about tomorrow, I just live from day to day. I don't borrow from its sunshine, for its clouds may turn to gray. Many things about tomorrow I don't seem to understand, but I know who holds the future, and I know Who holds my hand."*

That was another turning point. I can't say I never worried after that day, but when I did feel frantic, I kept coming back to the One I knew held my hand.

FOR THOUGHT, JOURNALING, OR SHARING

Whether medical, emotional, or relational, what have been your greatest challenges in caring for your loved one? Where do you turn for help, and how effective is that help?

It saddened me to see Tom's once confident personality fade. Many times during our marriage, I had wished he'd be at home more, or that he would spend more time with me. That wish wilted when it became reality. Someone has said retirement is half as much money and twice as much husband. Double that for Alzheimer's. I began to feel like his security blanket.

If I left the room, he'd call, "Where are you?" or "Are you okay?" He followed me everywhere, even standing outside the bathroom door until I came out and standing at my elbow when I was making dinner. I kind of liked it at first. He'd come up behind me as I was doing dishes or chopping vegetables, put his arms around me and kiss the back of my neck. Sweet.

"I love you," he'd tell me over and over. And over.

"I love you, too," I'd say. And I meant it. I felt ashamed that after a while I felt like saying instead, "Why don't you go sit down in the living room. I'll call you when supper's ready."

Oh, yes, I had often complained through the years that he didn't help out enough around the house. Now he wanted to help with everything, and really I appreciated it up to a point. Especially when I couldn't reach things on the upper shelves, and I'd call, "Tom, I need your arms." Or, "The dog needs to go out. Can you take her? I'm still in my pajamas."

Unfortunately, I always think there's a right way to do everything, whether it's making a bed, folding a towel, or putting away the groceries. Of course—you guessed it!—the right way was MY way.

For instance, doing the dishes. They either had to be loaded in the dishwasher and run through the cycle, or else washed in hot, soapy water, rinsed thoroughly, and air dried in the rack before putting them back in the right cupboard. Tom couldn't see the sense in that. If it was just a plate that had a sandwich on it or a water glass, all it needed was a quick rinse under running water, a swipe with a dishtowel that might also have been used as a hand towel, and a return to the cupboard. When I complained loudly, he would loudly respond, "Nobody's going to die because of the way I washed that dish."

As for the silverware being washed that way ... I shuddered to think what might happen to us if they were not sanitized. Once (or more) I even found a sticky spoon in the drawer or a knife with a smear of butter on the handle. I knew he wanted to help ... wanted something to do ... so I struggled and struggled to let go of my attitude, and finally took a deep breath and let it go, mumbling under my breath the words of Queen Esther going in to the king's chamber, "If I perish, I perish."

It was far more important that he was being useful and showing his love in a concrete way, wanting to serve and lighten my chores. Truthfully, his heart had not changed at all. All his life he received the greatest joy from helping others, and he still did.

Everyone needs and deserves respect regardless of how able or disabled they are. It's very easy to lose sight of that when you have to take care of someone else's basic needs. It's also easy to forget one's own needs.

I remembered when we were newly-married and still in college. We were almost always broke, but once Tom said to me, "I don't consider the cost of your going to the beauty shop a luxury. It's a necessity." I took him at his word and made an appointment the next day.

As Tom became more and more dependent on me for his daily necessities, I realized I also needed to take care of myself. I contacted our county Aging and Disability Council and arranged for in-home help. The first caregiver we were assigned was a middle-aged, efficient person. I was glad to be able to have a few hours to do errands, have lunch with a friend, or even go shopping. When I came home, the household chores were done, and I could give Tom all my attention. However, something was wrong. Tom was unhappy, and I could see why. She spoke to him as if he were a child and when he wanted an adult to adult conversation she continued to talk down to him. Obviously, she was the expert. I'm embarrassed to admit she was a bit like me, thinking her way was the right way. Fortunately, I was able to explain to the home care agency that this competent lady was not a "match" for Tom's needs.

Then, along came Terrie! What a blessing this upbeat, kind lady became to both of us. She treated Tom with the greatest respect, talked with him, laughed at his jokes, and did everything I asked of her. She even loved our dog, who greeted her joyfully with wiggles, barks of joy, and kisses. I could have kissed her myself. It's not just about the job. The relationship and understanding is the key. Terrie became a permanent and sweet part of our life.

Many other people also treated Tom with gentle understanding. One time we went out to eat with close friends. Having difficulty figuring out the menu, Tom had started either letting me order for him, or saying, "I'll have the same thing as my wife." But at the end of the meal, he still took care of the ticket. On this particular night, he was unable to figure out how to pay the bill. It was the first time that had been a problem for him. The men were sitting on the other side of the table, and his friend tactfully and gently figured out the tip and showed him where to sign. I so appreciated Dennis that night. A true friend is one who comes alongside you without calling attention to a potentially embarrassing moment.

At the apartment complex, Tom had made friends with many of our neighbors and was popular for his sense of humor and helpful actions. As they witnessed the changes in him, they showed their affection and support. When he got lost inside the building, they brought him home. If he went outside without his keys, they let him come through their apartment or unlocked the outside door for him. If he accidentally came to their door instead of his own, they would redirect him with a smile. They invited him to sit with them and visit, whether they had heard the same story ten times or not. If they saw him walking down toward the road, they walked with him and brought him home. People on the outside often said to me, "He's not safe! He's a danger to himself. You must put a lock on the inside of your apartment so he can't get out." I didn't ignore their concerns, because in part they were right. Especially considering that he had gone out many times while I was sleeping at night or early morning. Still, I couldn't bring myself to lock him in. Always a very active and restless person, Tom was always on the move. He didn't have the attention span anymore to sit and watch TV, and his anxiety wouldn't let him be idle. I did the best I could to keep track of his movements, but I had to sleep sometimes! I know that without the kindness and care of our neighbors, he would not have been able to remain living with me in our home. I am grateful for their compassion.

When you truly love someone, you have to let them be free to make their choices as much as possible. We know that's true about parenting as well as friendships. Why would it be different with your spouse, even if he/she does have Alzheimer's? Even if it's tricky to find the balance between protecting and joyful living? And it's good for me to realize my way of doing things is not the only way. Of course you'll make mistakes, but keep on saying "I love you," and just breathe.

FOR THOUGHT, JOURNALING, OR SHARING

How can you find balance in protecting your loved one, respecting his or her freedom, and taking care of yourself? What does "self-care" mean to you?

THE WORLD AROUND YOU

Most of the struggles of the Alzheimer's journey take place in your own home, but you do live in a wider place, and for good or ill you must interact with others traveling their own ways.

Just to get this out of the way, let me say that Tom's most difficult days coincided with the awful experience of the COVID19 panic in 2020. No, we did not become ill physically (thank God), but mentally and spiritually we shared the anguish that swept our nation.

Did I ever mention that Tom is a truly social person? He is probably the only person I know who prefers using a public bathroom so he has someone to talk to. (Allow me some hyperbole here.) When the lockdown began, our world shrank. Never having been especially good at remembering names, he always recognized faces, but not when the faces disappeared under masks. He walked the halls of our building looking for a friend and found no one. All the activities he had enjoyed such as potluck dinners in the social room, football fan gatherings in the media room, and casual chats around the fireplace were cancelled. He paced. In and out of our apartment. Up and down the stairs. Round and round the sidewalks surrounding the building. Thank goodness for the dog walkers and smokers who still could be found outside now and then. He often forgot to put on his mask or carried it in his pocket instead of on his face. People he did encounter reacted in several ways. If they didn't understand he had dementia, they would rebuke him. If they were kinder, gentler sort, they'd hand him a mask and remind him to wear it. In time, he wound up with pockets full of disposable masks. And I wound up feeling guilty because I couldn't keep my eye on him every minute.

Another loss came with the shut-down of restaurants. We were never fast food people, (except for blizzards at Dairy Queen) so going through a drive-through or ordering pizza was never a thrill for us. We did like to double date and enjoy a steak, a glass of wine, and leisurely conversation with friends in a cozy booth. Not that we didn't eat well at home, but we missed the friendship factor caused by stay-at-home rules.

Family time was also fractured by the governor's restrictions forbidding us to even gather for holidays, and Tom began to lose touch with our kids and grandkids, even forgetting their names. The only constant was the big family picture on our living room wall. He'd sit on the couch, staring at the faces, struggling to remember.

Worst of all was the cancellation of church services. No matter how forgetful he became in everyday functions, when we walked into the sanctuary of our church, he was restored to wholeness. He has a wonderful voice and grew up singing the majestic songs of our faith. I watched him standing beside me, singing "How Great Thou Art," with tears in his eyes and I got a lump in my throat. This was my love. The entire service was a spiritual feast. Exchanging the sign of peace with smiling people. Hearing the old, old story of Jesus and his love which is new with every telling. Even receiving the benediction and final amen before gathering in the narthex for coffee, cookies, and fellowship. That was our bread. It was tossed out by the need for everyone to stay home and be "safe."

How heartbreaking to hear him groan month after month, "Are we ever going to get to go to church again?" He began to pace the floor, praying aloud. "Lord, help me to be the man you want me to be. I'm so confused; I don't know what to do. I need you. Lord, help me." The pain resonated in my heart, too. I could only watch as he became more distant and farther from the life we had shared so long.

Under normal circumstances, routine helps the person with Alzheimer's to feel more secure and function better as a result. I had to find some way to restore the rhythm. Unfortunately, I couldn't replace the people or the atmosphere of the sanctuary, but I did find programs on television with the type of music he enjoyed and we watched those every Sunday. Our church had podcasts with the weekly service. It was kind of fun to watch our pastor standing outdoors preaching in the open air with birds singing in the background, or listening to the children's pastor telling a story from his living room with his own children interacting with the message. And, of course, church can be anywhere two or three are gathered in the name of Jesus.

"Come sit down, honey," I would say. "Listen to this."

And he would settle down across the living room as I opened the Bible and read to him. No words are sweeter to a thirsty soul than Jesus' call, "Come to me, all you who are weary and burdened, and I will give you rest."

Our "little church" brought peace as we waited for the doors of the sanctuary to open again.

Sadly, as the restrictions continued, Tom never did get to go to the church services again, but we continued to follow the routine of prayer and Bible reading, and our best and sweetest talks centered on the Lord.

I am reminded of the truth, "Though the outward man perishes, the inward man is renewed day by day."

I am convinced man is more than a body and a brain. Even when it is evident that the body is weak and the brain is failing to function normally, there is another aspect of life. The spirit--though unseen and unmeasured--lives vibrantly. Nourish it daily. One of my little boys used to wake up every morning when he was three singing, "This is the day that the Lord has made. We will rejoice and be glad in it..." What will you rejoice about today?

FOR THOUGHT, JOURNALING OR SHARING

As your loved one's world seems to shrink with the loss of function or changes in the world around you, is it possible to keep a spiritual focus in your relationship? Focus on the reality of God's presence and remember that no matter your circumstances, He cares for you.

Who hasn't lost something important at some time? Left your coat behind at someone's house? Searched high and low for an important paper? Gone crazy looking for your glasses or keys? Somehow managed to lock yourself out of your car or house? Raise your hand if you've never experienced any of the above? Okay, so there's one hand. You may be excused of struggling through life with the rest of us.

All of these events were common at our house, even before memory loss set in. We've always been on the go, chasing a deadline, leaving a trail behind us and trying to retrace it and find something we've forgotten. I got used to frequently helping Tom hunt for things, but with Alzheimer's it became a constant occurrence. He often put his things away "in a safe place" so he wouldn't lose them and then forgot where the safe place was or even that he had the item in the first place. He lost his identification, three separate wallets, glasses, keys, hats, and items of clothing on a regular basis.

For instance, I'd be doing laundry or other chores, and he'd decide to go for a walk. All of a sudden, he'd call, "Jeri, I can't find my key," and he'd go through our apartment opening every closet, rummaging through every drawer, and becoming more and more upset with himself. I'd stop my work, join the hunt, and ask stupid questions like, "When did you last have it?" which did nothing to reveal a clue.

Eventually, I'd rescue him by letting him "borrow" my key, holding my breath and praying he wouldn't lose that also. I tried putting the key on a chain fastened to his belt loop. That didn't help Iput a lanyard around his neck with his keys on the end. He came back without the lanyard, and the keys were lost again. I could write pages of similar stories, and I will have to admit that I did not handle the stress very well. I tried my best to be calm, not to blame him, and to understand it was not his fault that he couldn't remember, but at times I just felt like screaming.

And sometimes I did. I was ashamed that I yelled at him, but I was frustrated that I could not concentrate on anything without interruption.

Tension grew when he repeatedly asked the same question. "I just told you three times," I'd groan, dismayed by the hurt look on his face. I realized I was shaming him. *He tries so hard.* I reminded myself. Once again, a scripture flashed into my mind, *"Man looks on the outward appearance, but God looks on the heart." (I Samuel 16:7)* I knew Tom's heart. It was a good heart. A heart of love for me, for God, and for others. I needed to change my attitude, and only the Lord could help me.

An unexpected thing happened. As I spent more time reading the Word of God, I started to see my own faults. As merciful and gracious as God was to me, He could also give me the will to extend grace to Tom. Another funny thing happened. When I consciously made a decision to choose to love, I began seeing the humor in things that had irritated me. For instance, Tom had become obsessed with his feet, shoes, and socks. He constantly put his shoes off and on and took off his socks and put them in odd places. I found socks inside bowls on the shelves, draped neatly over the backs of chairs, wadded up in my closet. I never knew if they were fresh from his closet or had been worn a day or two, but instead of making a fuss over it, I just tossed them in the wash, laughed, and moved on. Sometimes I grabbed my phone and took a picture to send to my sisters, so they could laugh with me. I knew they loved him too.

Another habit he developed was picking up things he found lying around in the building and on the property. He appeared at our apartment with assorted objects: a lost coat, a newspaper from someone else's front door, an odd glove, a package of cookies, a hat, and a blue cane. Where did he find them? Nobody knew. He really became attached to that cane, and enjoyed taking it with him on his frequent walks. But one day, it disappeared. He had no idea what had happened to it, but when we went down to get in our car one afternoon, I saw the blue cane inside the car parked next to us. I assumed the owner had left it leaning against her car, and Tom had appropriated it for a while. One day he left it outside, and it had been reclaimed by the rightful owner. It struck me funny. Embarrassing, but funny. I laughed and laughed.

I'm telling you, if you have no sense of humor, you are doomed. There's so much in life you can't control, and if you take everything seriously you're making your life miserable.

There is a well-known proverb: *"A merry heart doeth good, like a medicine, but a broken spirit drieth the bones." (Proverbs 15:13 KJV)*

Certainly, there are many days of sadness and frustration coping with the decline of the one you love, but there are also opportunities to relax and let the sunshine in. Don't miss them!

Read the comics together. Watch old comedy shows. Talk about funny things that have happened in the past, and don't worry if your partner doesn't remember them. You can laugh at it anyway. I was very blessed that Tom retained his Irish sense of humor, and he liked hearing me laugh and smile even if he didn't understand the joke. Life can get dreary if you don't lighten up.

Think of a behavior or situation that wears on your nerves but isn't a catastrophe. How could changing your attitude make a difference? Did you ever have a situation when you changed your outlook and were able to relax and appreciate the humor?

WHAT TIME IS IT? WHERE ARE WE?

You know, if you are retired, that time moves differently. It's easy to forget which day of the week it is, because most days are the same. It's even hard to keep track of appointment times unless you write them on the calendar or enter them in the schedule electronically. (And then, you have to remember to check every day.)

A person with Alzheimer's has additional problems. He can't sense whether it's morning or evening or whether fifteen minutes or two hours have passed. The concept of sleeping all night and getting up in the morning becomes confusing.

For Tom, bedtime happened right after supper. He would get up from the table, thank me for the dinner, and start undressing. Since he ate faster than I did, I usually was only half finished with my dinner, had to bolt it down, and jump up to help him, or convince him it was too early to go to bed. "Why don't we watch a TV show?" I'd often suggest.

"Okay," he'd agree, and into the den we would go, turning the channel to old classics such as *Mash* or *Andy Griffith* reruns which held his attention for a short while. It didn't matter that they were re-runs. They were all new to him! When I'd go back to the kitchen, he'd jump up and follow me, trying to help with the cleanup. It made me so nervous!

Before long, he'd start getting ready for bed again, and need my help. By 7 or 8 o'clock, he'd be under the covers. *Ah, now it's my time to relax. Shall I finish watching that TV show, check my Facebook page, do a little writing, or settle down in the recliner and read awhile? Maybe a leisurely soak it the tub.*

None of the above.

He would call to me, "Are you coming to bed?" or get up and come to see what I was doing. He might sit by me, stare at the computer screen and say, "Who are you talking to?" When I was reading, he'd come to the living room and pick up a two-day old (most likely stolen) newspaper and start reading the headlines out loud to me. At last, I gave up trying to find "me time," and went to bed, hoping to sleep through the night.

That proved to be a vain hope. One night I woke up around 2 a.m. and he was gone. Just gone! I looked around the building and outside, but couldn't find him. "At least the car is still here," I thought. "He can't be too far away," and anxiously wondered whether to go looking for him or to call the police.

He did come back that night. He had gotten the idea in his head to go for a walk to the hardware store downtown, and came cheerfully home around 3:00. "Why?" I asked. Foolish me, expecting a reason.

From then on I slept restlessly until early morning, and then went into a sound sleep. I hardly ever heard him leave, but almost always I would wake up around 8 or 9 to discover he had been up for hours. Sometimes he took the dog out for an early walk and visited with the early risers in the neighborhood. Sometimes he'd be scrambling around in the kitchen making a peanut butter sandwich or eating cookies and ice cream. His idea of a healthy breakfast.

Often, he would be oddly dressed, picking yesterday's clothes out of the hamper or tucking a sweatshirt into dress pants. He might be wearing a jacket when it was hot outside or a thin shirt in the cold. I'd convince him to change. I don't know why I felt obligated to do that. Maybe it was because he had always been a neat dresser, and other women in our building often said to me how handsome he looked and I treasured those compliments. He was agreeable and didn't mind changing. I think he liked the ladies noticing him, too.

Not only was time a difficult concept, Tom often didn't know where he was. More than once the neighbor in the apartment above us was startled by her door opening and a man walking into her place. Fortunately, she knew Tom and was good-natured enough to send him home with a gentle word. She did begin locking her door, but he still came knocking at odd times. I couldn't understand how he could not recognize he was in the wrong place. She was quite a decorator and her entryway had all sorts of items that were distinctly different from the ones by my door. According to the eye doctor, there was nothing wrong with his sight, but he just was not making sense of visual clues. Before long, he became unable to tell time from a regular clock, and once in the doctor's office doing the mini-mental test to evaluate his skills, he was unable to draw the face of a clock.

That made me sad.

Worse yet, reading became difficult for him. Tom was always a reader. While I often enjoy a good novel or mystery, his taste ran to nonfiction, particularly Christian writers, magazines, and the newspaper headlines and sports section. Frequently we sat in our living room, each quietly reading a book until one of us would say, "Listen to this."

The other would stop to hear the passage read aloud, and then we would talk about it. We each read our Bible, too, but eventually he stopped reading much of anything. He tried. He stumbled over the words like some of the elementary students I had taught years ago.

We need words as much as we need food. We need companionship of shared thoughts more than we need food. When I sat down to read, I'd call to him, "Tom, come here. I want you to hear this."

He came and sat down across from me, and I'd read aloud. A beautiful description from a book I was reading. A poem. The words of a favorite hymn. Something I had written. A letter that came in the mail. Whatever it was, for as long as I read, he would listen. Sometimes we would talk about it and share our thoughts and reactions. Sometimes he would fall asleep. But in the hum of words, our souls joined as they had before. That hadn't changed.

There are many and drastic changes in a relationship when Alzheimer's is in the equation. Many times I felt like I was clinging to the flotsam of a sinking boat. Instead, I chose to cling to the still upright mast of the "love boat." Looking for the things that were still the same and making the most of the things that remained.

Not only did he enjoy my reading to him, but he liked going shopping with me, especially for our weekly food foraging—i.e. going to the grocery store or farmer's market. We usually chose to shop at the neighborhood grocery outlet. It was a smaller store, had lower prices, and the shopping took less time than trips to the big grocery chains. Best of all, we could take our dog Anouk into the store. Putting a clean towel in the basket for her to sit on, we wheeled her up and down the aisles and she sat like a princess enjoying the ride while we did our hunting and gathering. She's a tri-color Papillon, only the size of a new baby, and she attracted a lot of attention, giving Tom plenty of chances to make new friends.

He pushed the cart along behind me, while I filled it. Oh, he made sure to add his favorites to the cart as well and I usually came to check out with a number of items not on my list. He definitely did his part to make the trip easier, loading and unloading the groceries and bringing all the bags into the kitchen. I always made sure to thank him, giving him a hug and kiss and telling him how glad I was for his help.

He had almost never shopped with me before he had Alzheimer's, but now he always wanted to go, even if my friend and I were browsing for bargains at the thrift store. Also, he liked seeing my friends. If a neighbor dropped by for coffee and a chat, he'd pull up a chair and take part in the conversation as much as he could. Basically, he wanted to be part of everything I did, and I always felt that keeping him involved helped him stay in the present.

Part of the well-known serenity prayer asks for grace for "living one day at a time, enjoying one moment at a time, accepting hardships as the pathway to peace." Keep that prayer on your lips as you walk through the confusion and losses of Alzheimer's. It will lighten the load. There are so many things you can do nothing about. I am still learning to let go of expectations look for the good, for I know my husband is a good man.

FOR THOUGHT, JOURNALING, OR SHARING

Make a list of things that you and your loved one can still enjoy together. Think of new ways you can engage in meaningful relationship.

Do you have expectations you need to let go of to gain peace in your emotions? Which matters are truly necessary to keep? What is the first thing you say to yourself when you experience frustration with your loved one? What would be a better thought to replace it?

COMPLICATIONS

As Tom recovered from his heart attack, he continued seeing two heart doctors, one for the Afib. (Atrial fibrillation, meaning the heartbeat is irregular and too rapid) and another for other CAD (coronary heart disease) problems. He suggested Tom see a surgeon in Seattle about getting stents put in his heart. I wasn't sure how he'd deal with another hospitalization, but when Tom said he did want to have the surgery, we talked it over as a family and proceeded to go through the procedure, having three stents put in his heart.

The surgery took place on the day of our fifty-third anniversary. No hearts and flowers that year. I ate dinner off a hospital tray while my "groom" groaned upon a narrow bed.

He recovered well from the surgery at home, and even though the stents helped his heart condition, he still had to take various medications for heart, high blood pressure, and diabetes. I had to keep records of his numbers for blood pressure and diabetes and figure out when I should call the doctor. As much as I tried to keep doctor's orders about his diet, he loved his ice cream and other treats and would eat them all day long. Even though I felt guilty for not stopping him, I shilly-shallied. "There are so many losses and so many things he can't do anymore," I rationalized, "I feel mean depriving him of the one thing he enjoys."

Later, he had cataract surgery, which was very much a blessing, improving his vision to the extent that he no longer needed to wear glasses except for reading. He couldn't tell the difference between my reading glasses and his own, even though my frames were red and had sparkly little sequins on the bows. My, how cute he looked in those.

After getting an abscessed tooth, he had some teeth extracted and got a partial denture, a long tedious process with a lot of insurance forms and waiting. He kept asking, "When am I getting my teeth? I need them. How long is this going to take?" I kept explaining what was happening, but it didn't make any difference.

Also, his hand caused him constant pain. Just before he retired, he was working with a table saw and "he fought the saw, and the saw won." He lost a couple of fingers and had two extensive surgeries for a deep cut by his thumb and extending deep into the palm. Though he managed to function quite well, he had much pain from the severed nerves in that hand.

And, there's more! When he was struck by lightning years before (that's another story) his feet were quite badly burned. In addition, he never wore properly fitted shoes. By the time he retired, he had a bunion, a hammer toe, a fallen arch and a flat foot. (I suppose I am a sadist, but I can't help laughing at the last two paragraphs. It almost sounds unreal.)His doctors (God bless them) did their best, but he was clearly in discomfort with all these conditions, and his pain added to his confusion.

"I've got to get to the doctor and get this 'thing' cut off," he would say, taking off his shoe and sock and rubbing his foot.

"It can't be cut off," I would explain. "It's a bone in your foot from your fallen arch. Your doctor told you that at your last appointment."

The explanation didn't sink in.

"Would you like to soak your foot for a while in the foot bath? Or, I could massage your foot with that CBD cream I just bought."

He wasn't interested in that, so he put his sock and shoe back on and announced, "I'm going for a walk," and off he went. In a few minutes he returned. "When am I going to get my new teeth? I need my teeth?" and on and on it went.

The month of October was long and hard for both of us. I was thrilled when a good friend said to me, "Let's make a trip to the Oregon coast to celebrate our birthdays."

It didn't take long for me to agree to that plan. Our birthdays are only four days apart. What could be a better reason to take a break from all the responsibilities of caregiving.

We made our plans, and two of my sons and their wives stepped up and agreed to keep their dad and our little dog for four days.

Oregon is a beautiful state. Hills and mountains, big trees, rivers, a long Pacific coastline, and a great deal of history. You know, of course, about Lewis and Clark's famous exploration and all the tales of voyages of discovery, as well as the hardy pioneers who crossed the central plains to get to the fabled Oregon Territory. We had a great time enjoying the scenic drives, restaurants, farm lands, lighthouses, waterfalls, sea lions, and beaches. We even spent a whole afternoon flying kites on a beach and photographing the brilliant sunset. I slept well every night in the peace and quiet of our Airb&b.

I came home refreshed, ready to pick up where I'd left off and carry on bravely.

However, my sons had some news for me. Their time with their dad brought some surprising revelations.

"How do you do this, Mom?" they said.

They realized he did indeed have to be cared for round the clock. While I was away, his confusion multiplied and he was scarcely the dad they knew. Of all the incidents they told me about, the most upsetting took place one afternoon.

While Matt was working in his office, Dad decided to go for a walk. Without telling Matt, he left the property and walked half a mile down a steep road having lots of traffic, no shoulder, and deep ditches on either side. At the bottom, he turned down another busy road and kept walking.

Realizing he was gone, Matt anxiously searched his property.

Fortunately, our granddaughter Lauren happened to be driving home from work and spotted her grandpa. She pulled into the parking area of the coffee stand at the bottom of the hill and circled around to where he was.

"Grandpa, Grandpa! Where are you going?" She got out of her car and went to him.

"I'm going home," he said.

"Oh, no. It's too far to walk," she said, taking his arm. "Get in my car and I'll take you home." Though he didn't recognize her, she was able to get him into her car and drive him back up the hill to their house.

The next evening, Matt took him back to our apartment and was there waiting when I came home. He greeted me with a sober face and told me what had happened. From that point on, my family became actively involved in making plans for their dad's future care. and my need for help.

We agreed he needed more services and the social worker helped us set that up. He already had Terrie coming one afternoon a week, and They encouraged me to apply for more services and Terrie was able to increase her time four more hours a week. The other days and nights I was on my own. It was hard to find a good fit, and we began to consider moving him to a residential facility. Where would he go? He didn't need assistance with mobility; in fact, he had the opposite problem. He was a little too mobile!

He was still eating well and communicating his needs. He didn't need nursing care or hospice, but he might be better off in a place with people in charge who knew what they were doing. Or was it better for him to be with a woman who loved him dearly and spent every day and night by his side?

And yet, every once in a while a bright spot would shine through giving me courage to keep going.

One night after serving him a full steak dinner and a nice dessert, I asked him, "What was your favorite thing about this meal?"

He smiled at me and said, "It was all good, but my favorite thing was the pretty girl sitting at the table with me."

Oh, my heart! He might have dementia, but he sure wasn't crazy. What wouldn't I do for this man? Though the light at the end of the tunnel seemed dimmer by the day, I would not give up. Yet, in spite of my determination, I soon faced another crisis.

FOR THOUGHT, JOURNALING, OR SHARING

Have you ever wakened from sleep in a dark room and had a feeling of complete disorientation? Have you ever had that same feeling when dealing with the care of your loved one? When that happens, you, need, figuratively, to have a light by your bed to reach out in the dark. How can you prepare to find the help you need?

Nearly every day Tom complained of physical problems. I felt frightened when he often said, "I feel sick," or "My stomach hurts," but he usually couldn't tell me where the discomfort was. I could observe the sweating, anxiety and restlessness, but at what point should I take him to ER or call 911?

Surprisingly, the crisis came not because of heart problems, but foot problems.

That poor foot caused Tom such pain. He walked outside and paced the halls indoors all the time, and the pain in his fallen arch caused him to become obsessed with his shoes and socks. He was always taking them off and putting them back on, changing his socks and leaving socks in the oddest places. (By odd places, I don't mean behind the door or under the table. More like in a bowl inside a cupboard or on the top shelf of the étagère.) As for his shoes, he couldn't seem to keep track of them. Even the expensive pair of walking shoes I had just bought for him at a specialty store disappeared.

At his last appointment with the podiatrist, the doctor adjusted the arch support and told him to wear it for a month and then come back and see if it had helped. If it hadn't, maybe an orthotic shoe would be an option. However, Tom had not worn the arch support at all. He kept removing it and insisting he had to get the bone in his foot cut out.

The time had arrived for the follow up appointment. I was pretty sure there wasn't much to be done, but maybe the foot doctor could get him to understand surgery wasn't an option.

It was very early in the morning when Tom woke me up. He was in a panic. "You have to help me," he cried. "All my shoes are gone."

He stood helplessly in the middle of the living room with one shoe dangling from his hand. The room was a mess, with coats, clothing, socks, dishes, and papers everywhere. It was winter, and quite cold. I was supposed to take this man to the doctor, and he had not one pair of shoes to his name. I searched every corner of our apartment and couldn't find a single shoe. Even his pool shoes had vanished.

I sank onto the couch, and burst into tears. and began wailing.

"I can't do this anymore," I babbled. "I don't know what to do. I can't do this anymore. I just can't." I was getting hysterical and Tom was crying and shouting in confusion. I called my son, and as coherently as I could told him I needed help. He calmed me down and called his brother Jason (who lived closer) to come to my rescue. With their support, I got a grip on myself enough to call the doctor's office and cancel the appointment, and somehow we got through the day.

I understand now that it was not simply the missing shoes that caused me to fall apart, but the accumulation of months of stress and the escalation of fear. I lost my resolve to "be a good wife" in an instant. Certainly I couldn't find a shred of humor or even a crumb of grace for myself or him.

One of his missing shoes turned up in the dumpster a few days later. Apparently, he had taken it off outside and someone found it on the ground and threw thoughtlessly threw it in the dumpster.

When that was reported to the manager she took action. She went to the trash room, looked down in the dumpster and saw the shoe. Then, she actually climbed inside and grabbed it! Kelley, you're a hero!

The other shoes never did reappear, but I had to face the fact that I had to get help for Tom and for myself. It wasn't about whether or not I was a capable nurse/caregiver. It wasn't even a matter of loving devotion. It was about Alzheimer's disease.

And yet, I blamed myself. I had heard and read about people taking care of their loved one when the person became incontinent. Tom wasn't.

I had heard and read about people taking care of their loved one when the person became angry and abusive. Tom wasn't.

I had heard about people taking care of their loved one when the person became unable to communicate. Tom hadn't.

He still knew me, and every single day he told me he loved me. Any anger or fear he felt was directed at himself. One night he woke me talking in his sleep. "Fear, fear, fear," He kept wailing.

I now realize that Tom was sliding into the late stage of his disease, but at that point I just thought I needed to be patient and try harder, and try I did. I prayed daily for strength and grace as it became harder to understand him. He seemed like a different person. Instead of just helping him pick out his clothes, I had to help him put on the clothes and do the buttons and zippers. He needed hands-on help with grooming—bathing, shaving, oral hygiene and more. Sometimes he even needed to be guided to the bathroom or stopped from using the sink as a urinal.

Still upset by the COVID restrictions and isolation, he began insisting, "We don't live here. I want to go back to the United States." And he'd begin carrying things down to the car and set them on the roof of the vehicle. Once I looked out and saw a sack of potatoes, a boot, and some towels on the car roof.

One morning I heard him opening the door. He was coming in from outside. "Jeri, wake up," he said. "Do you know where we are?"

"Yes. This is our apartment. In Mount Vernon."

"Whose stuff is all this?" he gestured at the furnishings in the bedroom.

"Everything in here belongs to us."

"We'd better start taking stuff down to the car," he said. "so we can go home."

I knew we were speeding to a point of major change, but I didn't have time to think about it now. Thanksgiving was coming, and I had pies to bake.

Are you kind to yourself? When you feel like a failure, remind yourself that Jesus carries all your grief and knows all your sorrow. Take time today to do something that inspires you, whether it is reading a book, going shopping, going to the gym, or having coffee with a friend.

I love the line from C.S. Lewis's book, *The Horse and His Boy*. The discouraged boy Shasta says, "Sometimes I feel I haven't accomplished much." Horse replies, "You've got up and carried on. You are brave and magnificent."

SOME HAPPY HOLIDAYS

Thanksgiving Day was always a memorable holiday for the Tyner clan. When our sons were growing up, it was the traditional "Over the river and through the woods to Grandmother's house we go." All the cousins, aunts and uncles and random other souls gathered at the Glenn and Ruth Tyner home. All the ladies brought their specialty dishes to add to the traditional fare and Grandma's "sticky cinnamon rolls" got rave reviews. The competition for best pies continued year after year, as did one sister's insistence that we hadn't used enough water to cook the potatoes.

Nor did we forget to share our thanks for all God's gifts as each person gave a word of praise before Grandpa said the blessing. After everyone was replete with pie, the real fun began with tag football in the yard (usually in the snow), games, singing and the warmth of being together. This year would be no exception, even though our "kids" now had big kids of their own, and despite the nasty virus limiting social events.

And even though Grandpa Tom was confused about who, what, when, and where, he still knew why, and brought his appetite along. There was a wide choice of appetizers, but he passed them by and went for the sweets and candies no matter who tried to steer him to the savory side of the table. Oh, well. He was enjoying himself and that's what mattered. He didn't have much to say this year, and I felt sad at his lack of social interaction. He soon finished his main course and was ready to dig into the pies. He really had a sugar addiction, and I had just about given up trying to get him to eat a healthy diet. There were far more serious concerns. Somehow, I knew this would be our last Thanksgiving with Tom.

Typically, he was ready to leave as soon as dessert was finished. He had changed from being the last one at the party to restlessly wanting to go home as soon as he could. Before we left, we went out on the deck and out came the !phones as family groups lined up for pictures with me and Tom. Those photos would soon become treasured memories. As for Tom, by the time we got home, he had already forgotten the celebration.

I wasn't really excited about the Christmas holiday. I expected it to be a small, low-key occasion. We had already decided that our family gift exchange would be playing the white elephant game. I usually bought toys for the two younger children and made Christmas cookies for the teens and adult kids, but this year I didn't even have the heart to do that. Honestly, I was feeling sadder every day.

Then, a Christmas miracle occurred. At least it seemed like a miracle to me. I was standing in Jason and Kirstin's kitchen on Monday before the holiday, when "what to my wondering eyes should appear" but our son from Texas and his wife Michelle, son, and new baby boy! I was totally surprised. It was the first time we had seen the baby, and the first time we'd been with Andrew for several years. I immediately got that sweet baby in my arms, and there is nothing better than a new baby's presence to remind us of

73

our Savior being born in the dark night of winter the first Christmas. All of a sudden, the magic was back.

Our daughter-in-law Jennifer had arranged for a professional photographer to come to their place on Christmas Eve day and take family pictures of us all. Shelli, the photographer, was everywhere with that camera, snapping pictures faster than we could say "cheese." She got formal group pictures—well, not really. It's hard to get the Tyner gang to be formal—but she did a great job of catching the personality of each person and family group. That was a much better gift than the white elephant exchange! A gift that will last for years.

The week with Andrew and his family was also a great gift, but as I watched my son sit and visit with his dad, my heart was tinged with sadness, knowing he had come to say goodbye. Tom loved the baby. He always loved babies and children, no matter whom they belonged to. I'm not sure he realized that Gabriel was his grandson, but it didn't matter. He was delighted with the baby.

No one talked about saying goodbye, but there was a sense of shared sorrow, and what meant the most to me was the knowledge that this is what Tom and I had built. The reason we stayed together through hard times in our marriage. The joy of Christmas. The joy that is worth every struggle. The joy of family. And I knew that in the future when Tom was gone, I would not be alone.

FOR THOUGHT, JOURNALING, OR SHARING

How have your holidays and celebrations been impacted by Alzheimer's disease? Is it possible to simplify the details and still keep the spirit of the day? How will you keep your loved one from being overwhelmed?

THE STORM

After Thanksgiving, Tom's CAD and Afib worsened. One night when nitroglycerin failed to relieve his chest pains and hydrosis, I called 911. He was taken to the hospital, admitted, and taken to the third floor. He was not happy at all and his presence wasn't much fun for the hospital workers either. He would/could not stay in bed, kept trying to remove tubes and medical apparatus and leave his room. Ever since high school Tom had worked in hospitals as an orderly and/or a therapist aide. In his present condition, he didn't understand why he was in the hospital, and he got the idea he was working there himself.

He said to me, "How did I get the job here? Did they call me to work here, or did I just come in downstairs and get hired?"

Dismayed, I answered, "No, Honey. You are here because you were having chest pains, and the doctor wants to keep his eye on you. The nurses need you to stay in your room." But my explanation did no good. He still thought he needed to check on "his patients," and kept roaming the halls. He felt he belonged at the nurses' station looking over charts. He even tried to leave the hospital when he thought his "shift" was over. The hospital brought in a nurse assistant to be with him 24/7 and keep him and everyone else safe.

In a few days, he was ready to be discharged with new medications and instructions to keep track of his glucose level, pulse, and blood pressure. Before we left the hospital, all three of his doctors, the head nurse, and the social worker came in his room and stood looming over me with worried expressions on their faces. The scene sounds funny now, but it was frightening at the time.

"What are you going to do?" they questioned me. "You need to make some long-term plans right away. You aren't going to be able to keep him at home much longer."

Long term plans? I was stunned. Then, I panicked. What was I going to do? I was still in the pattern of getting through one day at a time. The social worker gave me a list of facilities, and I promised to start calling them right away.

I really didn't want to call. My long term plan was to keep him home with me until the end. With the Lord's help and my family's understanding, I thought I could do it. After all, he loved me so much he would feel betrayed and devastated if I put him in a facility. Besides, such places were expensive and we were living on a fixed and limited income. My initial calls confirmed there were few if any facilities we could afford. The places in our county all had waiting lists and I was told people could have to wait up to three years to move in. I had been foolish and unrealistic to neglect planning for the inevitable situation I now faced.

After his discharge, we took Tom to his primary care doctor for follow up. My son was with me, and his wife joined in the discussion via telephone. We talked with the doctor about discontinuing his medications except those needed for comfort.

We all knew how Tom felt about end of life care. We had that discussion years ago. We also decided to have a hospice evaluation, but because Tom was able to walk without aid, talk and converse fairly well, feed himself, use the toilet and do other activities of daily living with some assistance, he didn't fit the profile for their services. (Hospice usually doesn't step in until a physician deems the patient within six months of death.) He did qualify for more hours of in-home care, but we weren't able to work that out. Due to his many health issues and need for management of diet and medication, the best option seemed to be a place that had memory care.

I found that there is a shortage of facilities of that type in our state, and I suspect that to be true on the national level. Dementia has grown to an epidemic!

Family care homes catering to three or four people vary in quality of their accommodations and services. Larger facilities are often crowded and always expensive. I knew of one lady who had a person come and live in her home to care for a disabled husband, but that wasn't feasible giving the lack of space in our apartment. Several places we investigated had a waiting list up to three years. Most discouraging of all, the COVID lockdown and prohibitions caused huge challenges. We were at a stalemate. The only place to go was down on our knees in prayer.

As it often happens, when you pray about something, the problem seems to get worse right away.

One night shortly after Christmas, I had just fallen asleep when Tom woke me up, groaning and crying out. I ran to the living room. At first I thought he was having another heart attack, but it turned out to be urinary retention causing his extreme agony. It was the first time he had experienced this problem. After treatment at the ER, he returned home with a catheter in place.

That was the beginning of a frustrating cycle of medical and emotional crises. In addition to the daily task of having the collecting bag drained, he couldn't comprehend why he had to have this strange tube attached to his body, thus he would pull it out and have to go back to the clinic or hospital. My poor husband became more and more confused and disoriented, less and less engaged with living.

I was still sleeping at six o'clock one morning when I heard the door open and close. I ran to the door and looked down the hall just in time to see Tom disappearing down the stairs. I hurried back to grab a robe and returned to the hall where I found a lady resident leading him back to our door. All Tom had on was a T-shirt, and he was carrying the collection bag in a plastic pail.

My heart sank. This was truly the end. I knew it from the top of my head, through my gut, and to my wobbling knees as cold feet.

The next day, I got a phone call.

Over a year before, I had visited a memory care facility in our county and asked to be put on the waiting list. I wasn't in a hurry at that time, and I had almost forgotten about the place. Now, a new manager had come to the facility and was going over records. Did I still want to be on the waiting list?

His friendly, helpful manner encouraged me to tell him what was happening in our little corner of the world, and he gave me the name of a facility which had openings and the person to contact. Another godsend! Within the month, the details were resolved and our family came together to take their dad to a new place where he could get the care he needed.

Was it an easy decision? In no way. Did I feel guilty and ashamed? Yes. Did I tell myself if I loved him I would keep him with me at all costs? Of course. But it seemed to me a clear answer to prayer, and I moved forward with the wholehearted support and encouragement of my family.

When the day came for his admission, our oldest son arrived to "take us for a ride," and Tom willingly got into the car, not noticing the boxes and bags being loaded into the trunk. We traveled first to Dan's home where our two grandsons Brock and Cade hugged him and said goodbye. Dan's wife Delaine got in the car with us, and we drove to the facility where Jason and Matt met us.

It helped that the facility was beautiful, sparkling clean, and staffed by amazing people. After we completed the necessary documents, our sons brought in Tom's belongings and a staff member invited Tom to go for a walk with her. Each of us embraced him, and he accepted the hugs and kisses happily. I clung to the warmth of his body. My heart hammered when he reached out to take my hand, but the attendant said, "Oh, she's going to stay down here for now," and he walked through the doors with her and was gone, leaving me in an empty world.

Because of the restrictions, we were not allowed to go any further into the building. There was nothing to do but turn around and leave, trusting the people there would take good care of him.

About the people, they are the heroes along the Alzheimer's highway. They are knowledgeable, efficient, and above all, compassionate. Everyone has heard horror stories about nursing homes and care facilities, but our experience was nothing but positive. It must be a difficult job with little thanks or recognition, but those kind folks who do it will be rewarded someday.

I spent the rest of the day with my son and his wife, and then Dan drove me home. I had to get home to take care of my dog. She was glad to see me, and I picked her up, buried my face in her fur and cried.

It was a long, lonely night. I felt like I was in a small boat on a wild and stormy sea, tossed by waves of sorrow, relief, fear, guilt and doubt. I had no choice but to "put my hand in the hand of the Man who stilled the waters," and eventually, morning came.

81

Why is it that even when we know we have made the right decision, we second-guess our judgment sometimes? Does it help to have someone you trust reassure you, or is it better to try to handle your doubt alone?

WHAT ABOUT LOVE?

It's Valentine's Day. I've been having bouts of crying all day. I miss my Valentine.

My Tommy.

I don't know how this is even possible, but I got up in the night and walked into the living room, and I felt him there. It was as real as breathing. I swear his spirit was beside me. I flopped onto the couch and whimpered.

I didn't want this to happen. It's horrible to know the one you love can't come to you and you can't go to him. Horrible to know the one you love doesn't even know who you are sometimes. Doesn't know where he is, or why. Worst of all to realize you are the one who made the decision to put him where he would be safe so you could sleep at night.

I wonder if safety is truly the most important thing. What about love? The security of a warm hand holding yours? The strength of a shoulder to lean on?

Finding no comfort in my thoughts, I went back to bed. I could feel him beside me. So close. So warm. Quietly loving me.

King Solomon wrote, *"Many waters cannot quench love, neither can floods drown it."* (Song of Solomon 8:7)

Alzheimer's disease cannot destroy love.

FOR THOUGHT, DISCUSSION, OR SHARING

It was a surprise to me to learn that it is not uncommon to sense the presence or hear the voice of the one you are grieving over. Instead of telling yourself you are going crazy and trying to deny your feelings, allow yourself to do whatever you need to do or to feel as you process your loss.

"You.ve got to come and get me out of here! I love you so much, I can't live without you. You have to come!"

"I can't come," I answered. "No one can come in the building because of COVID. As soon as they lift the restrictions, I'll come to see you. You have to be patient. They will take good care of you."

That conversation was repeated many times in the first two months Tom lived in the memory care facility. I made it a point to telephone often, and sometimes he would ask an attendant to get me on the phone. I knew he was utterly miserable, and I felt utterly guilty. A failure as a wife. A selfish, mean woman.

Although I had the complete support of my family in moving Tom to memory care, and although I had believed the hand of God was at work in providing a good place where his needs could be met, I still cried. I knew that his deepest need was for love and assurance only I could give him.

Isn't it interesting that our brains and our emotions are so often in disagreement?

It was a good thing he was 55 miles away so I couldn't go running down there every time he wanted me. It was also a good thing (in a twisted sense) that COVID restrictions made it impossible for me to visit him in person. The facility did offer something called "window visits," where you could stand outside on the ground and talk to your loved one through a window.

I longed to see him, and after six weeks I thought he had adjusted enough to try the only option available.

I took our dog Anouk along. He loved her so much and loved taking her everyplace we went. He had walked her every single day the last five years, and he never sat down or lay down during the day or night without her companionship. When he went to memory care, she seemed very depressed. Dogs have an uncanny way of knowing the truth.

I was so nervous about going, I asked my friend Terry to drive us.

I checked in, and was instructed to walk around to the side of the building and wait for them to bring Tom down to the first floor.

The window was quite high above me. I am short, anyway, and I could barely touch the screen which was only open about five inches. When Tom saw me, he almost cried with happiness. Anouk went wild, whining and scratching at the screen in a frenzy to reach her pack leader. He tried to open the screen wider, but it wouldn't budge.

"Wait there!" he begged. "I'll come out to you." He whirled around and started looking for the way out. There was no way out. The attendant was at his elbow. "No, Tom. You stay here. Just say hello to your wife, and then I'll take you back upstairs." That's when I began to shake. I knew I had to leave before I collapsed. The whole visit had been a disaster lasting less than ten minutes. I returned to my friend's Jeep crying.

It's a good thing I didn't have to drive myself home. I couldn't have seen the highway through my tears. I felt like I had appeared as a frightening apparition, upsetting him and then vanishing. I made up my mind I would never do a window visit again.

COVID would have to end soon. Wouldn't it? I would wait to be able to visit in person. To touch him. To bring him a piece of homemade pie. To let Anouk lick his face.

I believe it was at that time that Tom started sliding into darkness. From then on, he lost his memory of me as his wife. It would be two months before I was able to see him in person, and by then he believed I was his little sister.

I usually delight in the coming of spring, but although the flowering cherry tree beside my balcony bloomed as beautifully as ever and the sun warmed my face on my morning walks, I seemed to only see the clouds. I moved through the days as if I waded through mud. Still, I kept moving. Sometimes all one can do is inch through the day.

FOR THOUGHT, JOURNALING, OR SHARING

The common phrase, "This too shall pass," is not much encouragement to a person grieving a great loss. Taking care of yourself in such times is vital. Make a commitment to yourself to stay well-groomed, eat right, and reach out to friends who care. See a doctor or counselor if you need to. What are some practical things you can do for yourself?

What do I do now? I ask myself. I ask that question almost every day. After 55 years of being married and after 5 years of living with a spouse with Alzheimer's, I am alone. I scarcely know who I am. As I grope for normalcy, I find that routine becomes my friend. I have a mental list of daily chores—make the bed (only one side needs straightening), clean up the kitchen (takes days to fill the dishwasher), clean the bathroom (the seat is always down), do a load of laundry (really only half a load), empty the trash, and so on. Keeping to a standard helps me keep going.

A new habit I've established is taking time in the morning for a cup of coffee and a salted caramel biscotti. As I settle into my favorite chair with my Bible in hand, my dog Anouk jumps up and snuggles in beside me. She shares crumbs of my biscotti, then goes to sleep, and I listen to her snore like a baby as I read my Bible and pray. I've never had this luxury before. I was always a "human doing"—taking care of babies, going to work, taking care of Tom, snatching a moment of prayer—and I feel my soul being nourished as I linger in this still posture.

I rub behind my dog's silky ears. She has been our pet for almost eleven years, and now that I'm alone, she is my reason for getting up in the morning. If I didn't have her, I could easily stay in bed all morning, feeling sorry for myself, but because she needs to go out for a walk, I have to roll out of that warm bed, get dressed, brush my teeth, comb my hair, and get out in the fresh air for some exercise. I meet other dog walkers outdoors, and greeting them reminds me I am part of a community. I am thankful for this little creature. I believe animals are one of the greatest blessings God has given to mankind. A pet can help heal your heart.

So can friends.

My friend Sandy who has experienced a deep loss in her life, called me one day to ask how I was doing. She caught me at a low moment, and I told her I was struggling with loneliness and confusion.

"Have you ever thought of going to a grief share group?" she asked. She told me she had found the support of such an experience helpful. "A new one is starting next month," she continued, "Here's the contact information."

I hemmed and hawed for a while, but eventually signed up and began attending. I can't say I bonded right away with any of the other attendees. *Nice people,* I thought, *but they are all dealing with losses by death. None of them have experienced the wounds of Alzheimer's in their lives. My husband isn't dead. I'm not a widow. I'm ... I don't know what I am. I don't know who I am.*

But I did keep attending the group. I guess because I am stubborn. I'm not a quitter. I grit my teeth and hang on.

One late night, though, I did feel like giving up. It had been a dismal day. Routine hadn't helped. The dog wasn't enough. I didn't feel well. I was mindlessly flipping through TV channels when I was gripped by increasingly uncomfortable pains in my chest. *Maybe I'm having a heart attack. Maybe I ought to call someone—let my friend down the hall know what's going on.* The tight sensation continued, but didn't worsen right away. *Oh, well. I'm not going to call anyone. It's probably nothing. If they find me dead on the floor in the morning, I really don't care. No one needs me anyway. I've done what I was put here to do. I raised my family. Had a meaningful career teaching. Tom doesn't need me. Doesn't even know who I am anymore.* The pitiful mood continued and I went to bed still in pain in body and soul.

But I did wake up in the morning feeling normal, and I scoffed at myself for my wild imagining. That evening, I went to the grief share group and sat there feeling dismal.

The usual people. The usual routine. As we came to the end of the video portion of the program, the group leader asked if anyone wanted to comment. I didn't want to comment, but something told me I needed to. *If you're ever going to get real, now is the time to do it.*

I cleared my throat and started to talk. "I feel like I need to share something," I quavered, and before I finished the next sentence I was sobbing. I told them how I had felt the night before and the atmosphere in the room changed. Not only did the others express their care and concern for me, but they became open and vulnerable about their own suffering. I felt cleansed. Outwardly, nothing was resolved. I still had to do the day to day work of grieving--cycling through the shock, anger, bargaining, depression and acceptance--but my perspective had shifted. I was ready to keep going, refreshed by love and sharing the hurt of being human.

FOR THOUGHT, JOURNALING, OR SHARING

Have you ever heard the expression, "Into each life some rain must fall"? Everyone experiences grief at many times. You can learn the stages of grief and steel yourself to not let it bring you down, but you can't know when you may be blindsided or how you will feel when it happens. The best thing you can do is to allow yourself to feel and respond. Do you think a counselor, a friend, or a support group could help?

HELLO AGAIN!

I'm on my way to visit my husband Tom. It has been three and a half months since we've been apart. He's in a memory care facility about 55 miles away. I have not been able to visit him at all because of COVID restrictions, but today I have an appointment for an in-person visit for half an hour. We've both been vaccinated, so they're allowing me to come. I feel very nervous, not knowing what to expect. I'm bringing him summer clothes (all marked with his name) a lot of toiletries, an electric razor (he lost the one he had there) and a boom box with a few CD's with his favorite types of music. I was going to make him a pie, but didn't. I also planned to bring Anouk, but felt like I had enough to manage without having a dog along. My friend Sue is driving me. I'm too nervous to go by myself and worried about driving down there. I'm thankful for her.

I'm at the door, going through the screening process. Presenting my vaccine proof. Answering questions about COVID19 symptoms. No, I don't think I'd be here if I had a fever, a cough, or vomiting. An attendant comes and lets me pass through the locked doors and go up the elevator. It feels like a very nice prison. I shudder.

On the second floor, I wait a few moments and the attendant brings Tom to me. Oh, he has changed. He's wearing clean clothes, but his shirt's a little wrinkled and his hair is long and standing out around his head like Thomas Edison. His eyes show confusion. He seems to have shrunk. Thinner and older. My heart sinks. I blink back tears. Oh, my Tommy.

He recognizes me and his face lights up. I go to him and we hug and hold on to each other. "Well, well," he says. "Look who's here. My little sister."

I swallow the lump in my throat.

"I have some things for his room," I say. It's only a few yards to his room, decorated in soothing neutrals and spotlessly clean. There are two single beds, neatly made, and a free standing, semi-partition between the two sides of the room. A small table with two chairs sits against the wall. Each side also has a nightstand and easy chair. Each has his own closet, and they share a nice bathroom. His roommate's name is Keith, and Tom tells me he's, "A nice guy, and we get along fine." I explain about the boom box and CD's and the attendant puts them in the closet. I hope they don't stay there. He won't be able to enjoy them without help.

We're led to a room called the library with about fifty books on a shelf and a table for eight. "This should be called the conference room," the attendant says. "Have a good visit. I'll be back in about half an hour." I run my fingers through Tom's hair, smoothing it into place, put my hands on his face and kiss him on the lips. He responds with surprise at such an affectionate embrace from his "sister," and we sit facing each other and begin talking. It feels awkward, as if we're meeting for the first time, but soon we are chatting casually.

He still has a catheter and the collection bag is fastened around his waist. He fiddles with it. "I need to get rid of this thing," he says.

"I have an appointment to take you to the doctor next week. Don't try to pull it out yourself. You'll just hurt yourself and they'll put it back in and make you wear it longer." (That's happened several times and it's a recurring problem.)

"Ok, then. If I try to take it out, slap me." He's so quick with the answer, we both laugh. He still has a sense of humor and quick wit.

He asks how I'm doing. "Where do you live, now?" he says. I discover he has no idea where he is or where Mount Vernon is. I pull out my phone and begin showing him pictures of people and places and sigh to realize his memory of our last five years is almost gone. I show him pictures of our family. He's very interested, but doesn't recognize faces. "Who's that?" he asks.

Finally, I come to a picture of our third son and his wife. "Matt!" he cries in excitement. "Who's he with?"

I move on to our family Marco Polo app and show him a video of our youngest grandchild, Gabriel, on his first birthday. Tom has a huge smile on his face watching the baby and comments with pleasure as the baby smiles and talks, but he has to ask who Gabriel is.

Pretty soon, he says to me, "I have a girlfriend. She's really nice. I'll go find her so you can meet her," and he leaves the room. I've been expecting this, because he has been telling me

96

about his girlfriend every time I talk with him on the phone. I've heard that her name is Ruth and I do want to meet her. He returns in a minute holding her hand and brings her in the room. She's about 5' 5", slender, medium length gray hair, and has a very kind face.

I have a queer feeling in my chest.

He introduces us and pulls out the chair beside him. As she sits down, I notice she is wearing a beautiful ring. I compliment her, and she tells me it's a black diamond. I extend my hand and show her the opal ring Tom gave me years ago.

"Oh, that's beautiful," she says. "I love the colors in opals."

"Tom gave it to me," I say.

"Oh, what a nice brother." She smiles at him. So I know he has told her I am his little sister.

"Yes," I say, "Tom is a very nice guy."

"He sure is." Ruth looks at him with admiration. "He's just wonderful. I love him. He's the nicest man I've ever known."

"I'm glad you are his friend," I say, and I mean it. I'm glad he has a lady to look at him with admiration, keep him company, and talk with him. Because of her, he doesn't beg me to "get him out of here." Because of her, he's adjusted to his new surroundings. Because of her, I don't cry.

The conversation continues for a while, and I show them both pictures of the dog, and Ruth admires her and asks her name. When I say, "Anouk" Tom remarks, "I used to have a dog named

Anouk." I smile. "But she's gone now," he murmurs softly.

He asks me again where I am living now and how far away it is. "I'm sure glad you came to see me. I hope you come again soon. Bring your husband with you next time. I don't think I've ever met him. What does he do?"

"He's retired now," I tell him, "and he is mostly just taking it easy these days."

"He sounds like me," Tom chuckles. "What's his name?"

"Actually, his name is Tom."

"What a coincidence," Ruth bursts out. And we all laugh.

I am getting emotional now. On the edge of hysteria. Apparently the attendant has forgotten about us, and we've been visiting almost an hour. I swallow and gulp a deep breath.

"Well, Tom, I've have some things for you out in the car. I brought you some shorts and summer shirts. I need to go get them and bring them in. I think it's getting near your lunch time, too."

"Great," he says. "I'll go down with you and carry them in." We leave the room, and Ruth disappears. "She's my girlfriend," he tells me again, gives me a meaningful look and says, "but we're not … you know …" and winks at me.

I go back to his room to use the bathroom, and when I come out, he's gone. A nurse with a cart stops me and I tell her who I am and why I'm there. She asks an attendant to go find Tom so we can say goodbye. Pretty soon, I see them coming toward me. "That's my little sister," I hear him say to the man beside him.

With a hug and a kiss on the cheek, we part. His helper takes him off to the dining room and I'm escorted to the elevator. I descend with a sinking feeling and arrive at the entrance. Sue and I bring in the clothes and leave them at the desk. After a brief conversation with the charge nurse, we say goodbye.

I am grateful to be with a friend. On the way home, we stop for lunch in Smokey Point. We have fajitas at the restaurant that was our favorite spot when Tom and I lived there. The place brings back many good memories. I sigh, sip my drink, and look out at the gray sky. It's probably going to rain again.

How would you define the word <u>grace</u>? If you act with kindness and love in a stressful situation, that is showing grace. It doesn't come naturally to most of us, but it is a god-given quality, and He gives us plenty of opportunities to "grow in grace." When have you sensed you are on the receiving end of grace? When have you had opportunity to give grace to another?

Since the beginning of the year, Tom has had a problem with urinary retention that has caused us both a lot of grief. The intense pain of being unable to urinate brought about a late night trip to the ER. The relief of a catheter was followed by more confusion and discomfort and it became an ongoing struggle to convince him not to pull it out. There is really no way to delicately describe what we went through. I tried to explain to the urologist he saw after the first trip to the ER.

> *Dear Dr. A;*
>
> *I need you to know some special circumstances in considering the care plan for Tom. He is an Alzheimer's patient and I am trying to make arrangements for him to be admitted to memory care because he is no longer safe in independent living facility. He has to be watched around the clock. He's even gone outside in the dark and can't get back in, and he doesn't understand or remember anything. With his primary care doctor's cooperation, as per our family decision he's been taken off medications except as needed for comfort. Since he was first seen at the ER, that night he cut the tubing with a kitchen knife and pulled out the catheter. When the pain returned, he went back to the ER to have a new one put in. In a few days he*

101

got up while I was still asleep and walked down to the lobby naked and lost, not knowing where he was and carrying the urine bag in a bucket. A kind resident brought him home. Since then I've had to constantly watch him, not even able to sleep through the night. I thought it would help if you were aware of these facts.

He had to wear the catheter eleven more days, which meant constant watching and regular emptying. Fortunately, a friend and neighbor who is a retired nurse assisted me with his care. (Thank you, Paula.) With her help and encouragement, he managed to tolerate the condition until the end of the month.

He was admitted to Memory Care with the cath in place, but he pulled it out once again and had to be taken to another urologist to have it reattached. Unpleasant as this topic is to discuss, it is just one of the realities of declining abilities of daily living for the Alzheimer's patient and caregivers.

Finally, the day came for me to pick him up from Memory Care and take him to yet another doctor at the Clinic.

Usually when I see my doctor, he walks into the room and says, "How are you today?" and I automatically say, "Fine," and then think, "Of course I'm not fine. If I were fine I wouldn't be here," and my brain kind of goes numb. So I decided that before taking Tom to the urologist, I ought to be prepared for an intelligent discussion.

Knowing little to nothing about kidneys and bladders, I went to the Mayo Clinic website to learn about Tom's current problem. I made lists of his medical history and symptoms, possible causes of urinary retention, and treatment options. I felt much more prepared to discuss the problem with the urologist.

The appointment went very well, and the three of us talked over each item on my list and decided what was best for Tom. He agreed to having the catheter stay in place and have a public health nurse monitor and replace it monthly.

I was finally learning how to be an advocate. Even when you are seeing a doctor for your own health issues, don't take it for granted that your medical professional has had the time to re-read your chart before he comes into the exam room. It's a good idea to prepare for the visit and make a list of everything you want to discuss with your doctor. I'm learning it's even more vital to do so when you are acting for a loved one. It can be complicated, though. It felt rude to me to talk about Tom as if he wasn't in the room and on the other hand, I knew he couldn't truly understand the situation. So, I tried to include him as much as possible, looking at him during the discussion and asking, "Does that sound right to you?" or "How do you feel about what the doctor is suggesting. Would you agree to follow that treatment plan?" Even though I knew he wouldn't remember the conversation, I believe he would feel he was respected and loved. It's easy to forget that just because a person's mental acuity has declined, he/she still senses caring and respect.

As we left the office and were getting into the car, I said, "How would you like to go to a restaurant and have lunch before we go back to your place?"

"Sure," he agreed.

I made the choice of a nearby restaurant and ordered for him. After he devoured the clam chowder, he began talking about his "girlfriend." I could tell her friendship was important to him, but I nearly choked on my French fry at the next revelation.

"She really likes to be kissed, and I make sure she gets lots of kisses."

What does a wife say to that?

I tried to respond as a sister would, being interested and noncommittal, but inside I was trembling. My heart was racing. We finished lunch and returned to the memory care home. I hugged him, and said goodbye.

At home, I dropped into a chair and held back tears. I had no idea how to process this new development. All I knew was a crushing sense of abandonment. I remembered a poem I had written to him years ago:

Daisy Petals

He says when I smile, I light up the room

(he loves me ... he loves me not)

Whether I'm wearing satin and lace, or nothing

He says I am beautiful

(he loves me ... he loves me not)

I'm the kind of girl (he says)

He'd like to see jump out of a cake

(he loves me ... he loves me not)

And he feeds me ice cream with a silver spoon,

 holds my hand

And kisses the back of my neck

And we're just getting acquainted after thirty years.

(he loves me ... he loves me not)

He loves me!

He has forgotten me! How can I bear such great hurt?

I decided to call his sister Anitarae—the one he believes I am—and told her about the visit. She shared my grief over this new loss and we both cried. Then she sighed. "When I was in kindergarten," she began, "I had a boyfriend named Jimmy. I truly loved him. We sat together and played together. We had nap time after lunch, and we would get our little rugs out of our cubbies, lay them down side by side on the floor, and take a nap. After school, we walked home holding hands, and when we came to the corner where we separated, we kissed each other goodbye. I loved him."

"All so innocent," I blubbered. "So sweet."

Thoughts of the first time Tom kissed me brought another bucket of tears. That was then. This was now. He had been a faithful, loving husband for over 50 years—a true and steadfast lover. All I could do was mourn the loss and know at this time his maturity was that of a child. To him, I was his little sister, and

Ruth was his girlfriend. They sat side by side, talked together, and he kissed her at the corner. Lots of kisses. Accepting that is very, very hard.

FOR THOUGHT, JOURNALING, OR SHARING

How does being another person's caregiver change a relationship? How would that role change in the relationship of sibling, parent, child, or spouse? In each case, how could you handle it?

AN IMPOSSIBLE DREAM

Summer rainstorms take me by surprise. You too? Maybe you're running errands or working in the yard or playing with your kids at the park. The day seems long. Your skin feels hot and dry and maybe you have the feeling of a headache coming on. Suddenly the earth seems to stop breathing, and then ... then you sense it. Wind ruffles your hair and the sweat on the back of your neck feels cold. With a stampede of clouds and a whip of lightning, the blessed rain rushes down.

One evening after Tom had been in memory care about six months, sorrow overcame me like a summer storm. I was whiling away a Friday night watching a movie on television, hoping some lighthearted entertainment would relax me before going to bed. In the movie, a character competing in a pageant came onstage for her talent performance and began to sing "The Impossible Dream." Almost everyone has heard that song made famous by the character Don Quixote in the musical *The Man of La Mancha,* and to me, that song holds special memories.

After being married eight years, Tom and I had just welcomed our second son and were working hard to build our life and keep from being overwhelmed by the ups and downs of life. Frankly, it seemed like the downs were winning.

We had become good friends with our next door neighbors, Pete and Maria. They told us about an experience they had which brought a glow back to their marriage and they encouraged us to go. "It's called Marriage Encounter. It's sponsored by our church, but anyone can go." Pete said.

"We'll set it up for you," Maria added, "and it won't cost you anything."

When we hesitated, she went for the win and overcame all our resistance. "We'll take care of your kids for you. Danny and Kimberly will have fun together, and I'd love to have baby Andrew in the house for a few days."

A weekend away by ourselves? What did we have to lose? So what if it was at a monastery sixty-five miles away and we weren't Catholic. They made the arrangements and we set off into the unknown.

We had a fight on the way to the retreat. Maria said we were supposed to bring a snack to share—cookies or chips or some simple finger food we could pick up on the way. Tom went into the store and came back with a couple cases of Pepsi. His soda of choice. Obviously because he didn't want to go all weekend without it.

According to Little Miss Know-it-all (me) that was not what we were supposed to bring. Certainly you couldn't call it finger food. Actually, I think I was just nervous about being "different," and in those days I still worried a lot about what other people thought. (Notice I gave myself the benefit of the doubt, but accused him of being selfish-and-stubborn-just-like-a-man.) I told him to go back and get cookies, but he ignored me and kept on driving.

It was such a silly thing to argue about; but then, that's how our fights began. Some small issue got blown out of proportion and pride kept each of us from yielding our ground. When we arrived at the monastery, we pasted on our happy faces, checked in, and he found a fridge to store his Pepsi. (Which incidentally turned out to be the most popular snack of all with the other husbands there. Much to my annoyance.)

Still feeling a little miffed with each other, we filed into the large room for our orientation. There were many couples there, all looking somewhat dazed and unsure. There was a mystical feeling of peace and expectation hovering in the room. In the monastery, there was a rule of silence—we listened to the presentations, but there was no discussion or conversation except when the couples were in the privacy of their rooms. The rooms were small and non-pretentious—no 'honeymoon suites' here!—and the meals (eaten in company with the monks) were simple. It was truly a pause from the rush of modern life, and—yes—peaceful.

The weekend turned out to be a life-changing experience. We learned, first of all, that our marriage is a vocation, a solemn covenant composed of a man, a woman, and God. We learned how to communicate and accept each other's feelings through a process called dialoging, and committed ourselves to practice it twenty minutes every day. Our ten and ten. Ten minutes writing about our feelings on a certain issue and ten minutes sharing what we had written. (Feelings? We were good at stating facts and opinions, but

110

feelings?) Accepting our spouse's FEELINGS and validating them without arguing brought an amazing change. I recommend it!

Woven through the whole weekend was the music from *The Man of La Mancha,* including the lyrics "The Impossible Dream" and the imagery of love between the idealistic knight Don Quixote and the kitchen wench Dulcinea. He loved her when she couldn't even love herself. His vision transformed her. He believed in light and courage and purity. And they gave themselves to the impossible dream that love can transform lives and people. Love is worth fighting for with your whole heart.

That's really not what we had experienced in the messages around us. In the "real world," you have to protect yourself from being hurt. Point out the other person's faults before he calls you out. If a relationship gets too hard, get out of it. Idealism is only for fairy tales and fools.

Yes, it's impossible. Yet, we are called to pursue it. *"Love is patient. Love is kind...Love keeps no record of wrongs and rejoices in the truth."* We hear those words often at weddings, but forget them when the glow of romance fades. At our marriage encounter weekend, we were called to take them seriously.

We came back to our friends and our children with renewed love and stronger faith than ever before, and were welcomed into a community of other couples (including our neighbors Bob and Marianne who became our lifelong friends) committed to renewal and encouragement. That was a special time in our life and it included (nine months later) the birth of our third son.

Years have gone by, and the dream has faded. I sat alone on a Friday night watching a movie and grieving.

"To dream ... the impossible dream ..." the clear melody rang out, "to try when your arms are to weary... to reach ... the unreachable star ..."

The memories ... oh! ... the memories. They surged over me and I couldn't stop weeping. What had happened to our impossible dream? Oh, yes. Our arms had grown weary and our star was more out of reach than ever before. How easy it would be grow angry that a cruel and mysterious disease had robbed us of romance and turned moonlight into mourning. Should I let go of the ideal and face the fact?

Grief is such a prickly bedfellow. It can overcome you with emotion and turn the world into long, wet blackness. But once in a while grief subsides into peace and understanding. I dried the tears. I grabbed at the peace. I let the truth bubble up. Despite ravages of time and fears of the future, I believe in the quest. There's still the trinity of marriage—the husband, the wife, and their Creator. God. The Eternal One who holds us in His strong arms when ours are too weary to reach for that star.

I pray for one shaft of starlight to shine in my darkened corner.

It doesn't come with a flash. It comes with a phone call

from Memory Care. Tom's legs are swollen. It's hard for him to put on his Levis, and he needs some sweat pants or loose slacks with elastic waistbands. And some soft, adjustable slippers.

"I'll have them there tomorrow."

Love is practical. Love is doing what needs to be done. That's the secret of the impossible dream.

FOR THOUGHT, JOURNALING, OR SHARING

Which losses caused by Alzheimer's have brought you the greatest pain and fear? Should you just block those feelings out of your thoughts, run away from them, or rehearse the pain over and over. Is there any way to process them and arrive at peace?

I just came back from walking the dog when my phone rang. The person calling told me that Tom had been taken to the ER because he was having trouble breathing, on top of ongoing problems with blood pressure, rash on his extremities, sores, swelling and more. They had my name as DPOA as well as his end of life directive (DNR) and they asked me what I wanted them to do. Oxygen? X-rays? Admission?

How can a person make those decisions from a distance of fifty miles away? I knew I had to get there as soon as possible.

I am blessed with a daughter-in-law who is an RN, as well as a truly amazing woman. I called her, drove to her house, and she and my son took me to the hospital. I knew I could count on Jennifer for advice and action. Because of her influence, I was allowed (despite COVID rules) to go into the emergency room to see Tom and consult with the doctors. She stayed by my side, and knew the right questions to ask and understood the answers. She also had been a major part of a family meeting with all the brothers and their wives before Tom went into memory care. We all knew Tom's wishes not to have his life artificially prolonged and his desire to go home to heaven when God called him. There was no question that we wanted him to be as comfortable and pain free as possible, as we struggled with our own issues with death of a dearly loved husband, father, grandfather, brother, and friend.

In his confusion, Tom wasn't able to fully grasp all that was going on or the seriousness of his condition, but one thing he did know: he did not want to be in that hospital or any other! He made that very clear to everyone as he struggled to free himself from wires and tubes and get off the bed. He was fighting for every breath, and Jenni did her best to quiet him even as she talked with the social worker and doctor to come up with a treatment plan. I tried to participate, but my heart was beating fast as I struggled to control my emotions, and she did the majority of the talking, though being conscientious to include me.

I don't know how long we were actually there. Time seemed to creep, then rush forward, then stand still altogether.

As we held Tom's hands and calmed him, a wonderful thing happened. His mind cleared, and he began to pray aloud, talking to his Maker as if He were right beside him. He looked at Jenni and told her how much he loved her. He kissed her hands and face.

"I love you, too, Dad," she said. "It's been almost 27 years since I've been your bonus daughter."

Then, he looked at me, and I saw recognition light up his face. For months, every time he saw me, he had called me his "little sister," (which wasn't a bad thing) but now he saw me. Me. Jerilyn. His wife.

Tom has always loved music, loved to sing, and loved the "oldies" songs from our teenage years. Jenni found the station on her phone, and soon the golden tones of Elvis Presley's voice filled the room.

"Love me tender, love me true all my dreams fulfill…"

Despite the mighty struggle to breathe, Tom started to sing along. He only made it through those six words, and then he pulled himself toward me, holding me as close as he could. He looked into my eyes and said, "I've loved you for a long, long time." He sank back on the bed, and I managed to say, "I know you have, and I love you, too."

He was not admitted to the hospital. With Jenni's help, we were able to arrange hospice care for him, and that evening he returned to memory care, which he now recognized as his home.

The next day was difficult, as his health continued to fail. Hospice came and attended to his needs. Family members were able to visit, and Sunday our oldest son and his wife and son went to visit. Tom had returned to his confused state, hunched in a wheelchair with his head bowed low over his chest and his eyes closed. He didn't respond to his visitors until Dan said, "Dad, how about a blizzard?"

At the mention of his favorite treat, Tom's head came up. "Oh, that sounds good."

So, of course Dan went to the nearest DQ and returned with a turtle blizzard. As Tom enjoyed his ice cream, Dan reminded him of days when they had shared a half gallon of pecan cluster ice cream together, and grandson Brock picked up his cell phone and recorded the scene with Grandpa Tom eating his blizzard.

Another day passed with increased medication and decreased function, and we all sensed the end was very near. Daughter-in-law Delaine and grandson Bishop went to watch over him. The next day, a friend drove me down to visit him, and I took along an overnight bag, prepared to stay nearby if it seemed prudent.

It seemed to me his breathing was not quite as labored as it had been, but he was so very weak my heart hurt for him. Again, he was very agitated. He would not lie down, and kept trying to stand up but was too weak. My friend Dawn and I wheeled him down the hall and into a sunny room with a great view of the blue sky, trees, and traffic passing by. "Well, look at that!" he enthused as we brought him to the window. Once again, we turned on the tunes, and he relaxed as favorite memories washed over him. I massaged his neck and shoulders and talked to him. Whether he understood or not, he knew my voice and found comfort. Other people who lived in the memory care were drawn by the music and drifted in and out of the room. One by one, they came to talk to him with gentle concern. "How are ya doin' today Tom?" "You behaving yourself?" "How do ya like that music? Makes ya feel young, don't it?" Two ladies kissed him on the cheek.

He is so loved, I thought. *He'll never be alone.*

I didn't spend the night after all. I came home. I ate my first meal in several days. I slept through the night.

Tom is still with us, and the Lord knows the hour when his earthly journey will end.

I have come to the end of this horrible, hard, yet beautiful journey of loving and living with Alzheimer's. I hope my words may be an encouragement for whatever path you are traveling.

God is real. Love is true. Live with courage.

AFTERWORD

Four days after the last entry, the Lord called Tom home. I had spent his last day and night with him, and he was released from his suffering around 1 p.m. We celebrated his life with family and dear friends at our church. Even as we grieve, our memories of him continue to be a blessing.

Thank you for reading my story.

I welcome you to contact me at jerilyntyner@gmail.com or my facebook page, Jerilyn J. Tyner, Author.

TWENTY-THIRD PSALM

The LORD is my shepherd; I shall not want.

He maketh me to lie down in green pastures; he leadeth me

beside the still waters.

He restoreth my soul; he leadeth me in the paths of

righteousness for his name's sake.

Yea, though I walk through the valley of the shadow of

death,

I will fear no evil: for thou art with me;

thy rod and thy staff they comfort me.

Thou preparest a table before me in the presence of mine

enemies;

thou anointest my head with oil; my cup runneth over.

Surely goodness and mercy shall follow me all the days of

my life;

And I shall dwell in the house of the Lord forever.

Authorized King James Version

Made in United States
Troutdale, OR
03/01/2025

29382384R00070